KEEP
CALM
AT
CHRISTMAS

For Esme, Clara and Toby,
who love Christmas

KEEP CALM

AT

CHRISTMAS

GOOD ADVICE FOR CHRISTMAS TIME

EBURY
PRESS

1 3 5 7 9 10 8 6 4 2

First published in 2011 by Ebury Press, an imprint of Ebury Publishing
A Random House Group company

The Random House Group Limited Reg. No. 954009

Addresses for companies within the Random House Group can be
found at www.randomhouse.co.uk

A CIP catalogue record for this book is available
from the British Library

The Random House Group Limited supports The Forest Stewardship
Council (FSC®), the leading international forest certification
organisation. Our books carrying the FSC label are printed on FSC®
certified paper. FSC is the only forest certification scheme endorsed
by the leading environmental organisations, including Greenpeace.
Our paper procurement policy can be found at
www.randomhouse.co.uk/environment

Printed and bound by CPI Group (UK) Ltd, Croydon, CR0 4YY

ISBN 9780091946555

To buy books by your favourite authors and register for offers visit
www.randomhouse.co.uk

A CHRISTMAS GAMBOL OFT COULD CHEER THE POOR MAN'S HEART THROUGH HALF THE YEAR.

Sir Walter Scott

CONTENTS

The turkey

Food

Drink

Overindulgence

Christmas TV

Goodwill to all men

Bah humbug

Comfort and joy

Religion

Spirit of Christmas

New Year

INTRODUCTION

Christmas comes but once a year, goes the old saying – even if it does now appear to begin in late September and carry on into the first weeks of the New Year. This early arrival and late departure, driven by the financial concerns of greedy merchants, is meat and drink to certain kind of curmudgeon. Despite their protests at the deplorable commercialisation of Christmas, they take secret joy in spotting its ever-earlier arrival, probably plotting the dates on a spreadsheet and exploring the correlations between the premature arrival of tinsel in the shops and the lack of backbone in the nation's youth.

The traditional nativity scene, with the infant and mother centre stage surrounded by shepherds, wise men and lowing cattle (Joseph lurking at the back looking a bit embarrassed; turns out he's not even the real father), is still one that most of us recognise. Anyone acquainted with young children will have seen the Christmas story played out simply and movingly, often enhanced with supporting characters puzzlingly absent from the Gospels: talking mice, stable-dwelling lobsters and even Bethlehem-bound ninja turtles.

Somewhere in the tangle of Christmas lies its religious, dogmatic heart: do you follow the creed of Delia, Jamie or Gordon when it comes to cooking the turkey? Eating and drinking to excess, as demanded by convention, is a key element to a satisfactory Yule. Apart from Christmas morning, stag parties are the only other legitimate occasions when it is considered good form to start drinking at breakfast. Gorging throughout the day before descending into a food- and alcohol-induced coma around late afternoon, from which one is roused in the time-honoured custom of an invitation to play charades, is the shape of Christmas for many.

But beneath the hype, the relentless merchandising, the fake snow and the sound of Slade echoing through every shopping centre in Britain, the magic of Christmas is still there. Why else would we put so much effort into getting it right, and be so disappointed if it flops, if deep down we didn't still have a splinter of the excitement and wonder of the Christmases of childhood in our hearts? We still all hope for the innocent pleasure of a white Christmas, just like the ones we probably never really knew. We have an image of what the perfect Christmas should be like and we cleave to the idea, even as we slope into the bookies for a bet on whether a snowflake will fall on the Met Office roof on the 25th December.

Nonetheless, it seems that whatever we throw at Christmas, it still comes through with its old magic and promise of a respite from the daily grind, and a time to appreciate the things that really matter. Like friends, family, and the *Morecambe and Wise Christmas Special*. So use the advice of this little tome to steel yourself for the stress-inducing marathon that awaits. Keep Calm and Merry Christmas.

CHRISTMAS

A MERRY CHRISTMAS TO EVERYBODY! A HAPPY NEW YEAR TO ALL THE WORLD!

Charles Dickens

I HEARD THE BELLS ON CHRISTMAS DAY. THEIR OLD FAMILIAR CAROLS PLAY. AND WILD AND SWEET THE WORDS REPEAT. OF PEACE ON EARTH GOODWILL TO MEN.

Henry Wadsworth Longfellow

CHRISTMAS IS A NECESSITY. THERE HAS TO BE AT LEAST ONE DAY OF THE YEAR TO REMIND US THAT WE'RE HERE FOR SOMETHING ELSE BESIDES OURSELVES.

Eric Sevareid

IT IS CHRISTMAS IN THE HEART THAT PUTS CHRISTMAS IN THE AIR.

W T Ellis

CHRISTMAS IS THE DAY THAT HOLDS ALL TIME TOGETHER.

Alexander Smith

WORK

WHEN A MAN TELLS YOU THAT HE GOT RICH THROUGH HARD WORK, ASK HIM: 'WHOSE?'

Don Marquis

I HAVE YET TO HEAR A MAN ASK FOR ADVICE ON HOW TO COMBINE MARRIAGE AND A CAREER.

Gloria Steinem

ONE OF THE SYMPTOMS OF AN APPROACHING NERVOUS BREAKDOWN IS THE BELIEF THAT ONE'S WORK IS TERRIBLY IMPORTANT.

Bertrand Russell

BY WORKING FAITHFULLY EIGHT HOURS A DAY, YOU MAY EVENTUALLY GET TO BE A BOSS AND WORK TWELVE HOURS A DAY.

Robert Frost

HARD WORK NEVER KILLED ANYBODY, BUT WHY TAKE A CHANCE?

Edgar Bergen

I LIKE WORK; IT FASCINATES ME. I CAN SIT AND LOOK AT IT FOR HOURS.

Jerome K Jerome

A LIFE SPENT IN CONSTANT LABOR IS A LIFE WASTED, SAVE A MAN BE SUCH A FOOL AS TO REGARD A FULSOME OBITUARY NOTICE AS AMPLE REWARD.

George Jean Nathan

FAR FROM IDLENESS BEING THE ROOT OF ALL EVIL, IT IS RATHER THE ONLY TRUE GOOD.

Soren Kierkegaard

A GOOD RULE OF THUMB
IS IF YOU'VE MADE IT
TO THIRTY-FIVE AND
YOUR JOB STILL
REQUIRES YOU TO WEAR
A NAME TAG, YOU'VE
MADE A SERIOUS
VOCATIONAL ERROR.

Dennis Miller

THE BEST TIME TO START
THINKING ABOUT YOUR
RETIREMENT IS BEFORE
THE BOSS DOES.

Anon

NEVER WORK JUST FOR MONEY OR FOR POWER. THEY WON'T SAVE YOUR SOUL OR HELP YOU SLEEP AT NIGHT.

Marian Wright Edelman

LAZINESS MAY APPEAR ATTRACTIVE, BUT WORK GIVES SATISFACTION.

Anne Frank

NOT ONLY IS WOMEN'S WORK NEVER DONE, THE DEFINITION KEEPS CHANGING.

Anon

AS IT TURNS OUT, SOCIAL SCIENTISTS HAVE ESTABLISHED ONLY ONE FACT ABOUT SINGLE WOMEN'S MENTAL HEALTH: EMPLOYMENT IMPROVES IT.

Susan Faludi

IN POLITICS, IF YOU WANT ANYTHING SAID, ASK A MAN – IF YOU WANT ANYTHING DONE, ASK A WOMAN.

Margaret Thatcher

TAKE YOUR WORK SERIOUSLY, BUT NEVER YOURSELF.

Dame Margot Fonteyn

YOU CAN FOOL ALL OF THE PEOPLE SOME OF THE TIME, AND SOME OF THE PEOPLE ALL OF THE TIME. AND THAT'S SUFFICIENT.

Rose King

LIVE NEITHER IN THE PAST NOR IN THE FUTURE, BUT LET EACH DAY'S WORK ABSORB YOUR ENTIRE ENERGIES, AND SATISFY YOUR WIDEST AMBITION.

Sir William Osler

IF YOU THINK YOUR BOSS IS STUPID, REMEMBER: YOU WOULDN'T HAVE A JOB IF HE WAS ANY SMARTER.

Albert A Grant

BY WORKING FAITHFULLY EIGHT HOURS A DAY, YOU MAY EVENTUALLY GET TO BE A BOSS AND WORK TWELVE HOURS A DAY.

Robert Frost

HOLIDAYS

IT IS THE ONE SEASON OF
THE YEAR WHEN WE CAN
LAY ASIDE ALL GNAWING
WORRY, INDULGE IN
SENTIMENT WITHOUT
CENSURE, ASSUME THE
CAREFREE FAITH OF
CHILDHOOD, AND JUST PLAIN
'HAVE FUN.' WHETHER THEY
CALL IT YULETIDE, NOEL,
WEINACHTEN, OR
CHRISTMAS, PEOPLE
AROUND THE EARTH THIRST
FOR ITS REFRESHMENT AS
THE DESERT TRAVELLER
FOR THE OASIS.

D D Monroe

I ONCE WANTED TO BECOME AN ATHEIST, BUT I GAVE UP – THEY HAVE NO HOLIDAYS.

Henry Youngman

NOTHING SAYS HOLIDAYS, LIKE A CHEESE LOG.

Ellen DeGeneres

BESIDES THE NOBLE ART
OF GETTING THINGS
DONE, THERE IS A
NOBLER ART OF LEAVING
THINGS UNDONE. THE
WISDOM OF LIFE
CONSISTS IN THE
ELIMINATION OF
NONESSENTIALS.

Lin Yutang

TAKE REST; A FIELD THAT
HAS RESTED GIVES A
BOUNTIFUL CROP.

Ovid

THE REAL PROBLEM OF LEISURE TIME IS HOW TO KEEP OTHERS FROM USING YOURS.

Arthur Lacey

YOUR MIND WILL ANSWER MOST QUESTIONS IF YOU LEARN TO RELAX AND WAIT FOR THE ANSWER.

William S Burroughs

**GENERALLY SPEAKING,
EVERYONE IS MORE
INTERESTING DOING
NOTHING THAN
DOING ANYTHING.**

Gertrude Stein

**FOR FAST-ACTING
RELIEF, TRY
SLOWING DOWN.**

Lily Tomlin

THERE IS NO PLEASURE IN HAVING NOTHING TO DO; THE FUN IS HAVING LOTS TO DO AND NOT DOING IT.

Mary Wilson Little

PARTIES

CHRISTMAS IS A TIME WHEN EVERYBODY WANTS HIS PAST FORGOTTEN AND HIS PRESENT REMEMBERED. WHAT I DON'T LIKE ABOUT OFFICE CHRISTMAS PARTIES IS LOOKING FOR A JOB THE NEXT DAY.

Phyllis Diller

NO MAN DOES RIGHT BY A WOMAN AT A PARTY.

Harry Golden

HEAR NO EVIL, SPEAK NO EVIL – AND YOU'LL NEVER BE INVITED TO A PARTY.

Oscar Wilde

AT EVERY PARTY THERE ARE TWO KINDS OF PEOPLE — THOSE WHO WANT TO GO HOME AND THOSE WHO DON'T. THE TROUBLE IS, THEY ARE USUALLY MARRIED TO EACH OTHER.

Ann Landers

NEVER BE THE FIRST TO ARRIVE AT A PARTY OR THE LAST TO GO HOME, AND NEVER, EVER BE BOTH.

David Brown

A DOG IS FOR LIFE, NOT JUST FOR CHRISTMAS. SO BE CAREFUL AT THE OFFICE CHRISTMAS PARTY.

Jimmy Carr

AT THE OFFICE PARTY YOU'RE SUPPOSED TO SIT NAKED ON TOP OF THE PHOTOCOPIER, NOT THE SHREDDER.

David Letterman

THE OPPOSITE OF TALKING ISN'T LISTENING. THE OPPOSITE OF TALKING IS WAITING.

Fran Lebowitz

PLAINNESS HAS ITS PECULIAR TEMPTATIONS QUITE AS MUCH AS BEAUTY.

George Eliot

A GOSSIP IS SOMEONE WHO TALKS TO YOU ABOUT OTHERS, A BORE IS SOMEONE WHO TALKS TO YOU ABOUT HIMSELF, AND A BRILLIANT CONVERSATIONALIST IS ONE WHO TALKS TO YOU ABOUT YOURSELF.

Lisa Kirk

IF PASSION DRIVES YOU, LET REASON HOLD THE REINS.

Benjamin Franklin

THE REAL ART OF CONVERSATION IS NOT ONLY TO SAY THE RIGHT THING IN THE RIGHT PLACE BUT TO LEAVE UNSAID THE WRONG THING AT THE TEMPTING MOMENT.

Lady Dorothy Nevill

DRESS IS AT ALL TIMES A FRIVOLOUS DISTINCTION, AND EXCESSIVE SOLICITUDE ABOUT IT OFTEN DESTROYS ITS OWN AIM.

Jane Austen

YOU CAN TAKE NO CREDIT FOR BEAUTY AT SIXTEEN. BUT IF YOU ARE BEAUTIFUL AT SIXTY, IT WILL BE YOUR SOUL'S OWN DOING.

Marie Stopes

BEAUTY IS THE FIRST PRESENT NATURE GIVES TO WOMEN AND THE FIRST IT TAKES AWAY.

Fay Weldon

A DRESS MAKES NO SENSE UNLESS IT INSPIRES MEN TO WANT TO TAKE IT OFF YOU.

Françoise Sagan

FASHION CAN BE BOUGHT. STYLE ONE MUST POSSESS.

Edna Woolman Chase

I'M TIRED OF ALL THIS NONSENSE ABOUT BEAUTY BEING ONLY SKIN-DEEP. THAT'S DEEP ENOUGH. WHAT DO YOU WANT, AN ADORABLE PANCREAS?

Jean Kerr

DO NOT WORRY ABOUT AVOIDING TEMPTATION. AS YOU GROW OLDER IT WILL AVOID YOU.

Joey Adams

LEAD US NOT INTO TEMPTATION. JUST TELL US WHERE IT IS; WE'LL FIND IT.

Sam Levenson

HOW LIKE HERRINGS AND ONIONS OUR VICES ARE IN THE MORNING AFTER WE HAVE COMMITTED THEM.

Samuel Taylor Coleridge

SHOPPING

FROM A COMMERCIAL POINT OF VIEW, IF CHRISTMAS DID NOT EXIST IT WOULD BE NECESSARY TO INVENT IT.

Katharine Whitehorn

TO PERCEIVE CHRISTMAS THROUGH ITS WRAPPINGS BECOMES MORE DIFFICULT WITH EVERY YEAR.

E B White

ONCE AGAIN, WE COME TO THE HOLIDAY SEASON, A DEEPLY RELIGIOUS TIME THAT EACH OF US OBSERVES, IN HIS OWN WAY, BY GOING TO THE MALL OF HIS CHOICE.

Dave Barry

IF MEN LIKED SHOPPING, THEY'D CALL IT RESEARCH.

Cynthia Nelms

A CHRISTMAS SHOPPER'S COMPLAINT IS ONE OF LONG-STANDING.

Anon

EXPENSE

**ABOUT ALL YOU
CAN DO IS DREAM
OF A WHITE CHRISTMAS,
FOR IT SEEMS LIKE IT
ALWAYS LEAVES MOST
OF US IN THE RED.**

Anon

**OH, FOR THE GOOD OLD
DAYS WHEN PEOPLE
WOULD STOP CHRISTMAS
SHOPPING WHEN THEY
RAN OUT OF MONEY.**

Anon

**CHRISTMAS IS THE TIME
WHEN KIDS TELL SANTA
WHAT THEY WANT AND
ADULTS PAY FOR IT.
DEFICITS ARE WHEN
ADULTS TELL
GOVERNMENT WHAT
THEY WANT AND THEIR
KIDS PAY FOR IT.**

Robert Lamm

**WHATEVER YOU HAVE,
SPEND LESS.**

Dr Johnson

THE CHRISTMAS SEASON HAS COME TO MEAN THE PERIOD WHEN THE PUBLIC PLAYS SANTA CLAUS TO THE MERCHANTS.

John Andrew Holmes

MANY BANKS HAVE A NEW KIND OF CHRISTMAS CLUB IN OPERATION. THE NEW CLUB HELPS YOU SAVE MONEY TO PAY FOR LAST YEAR'S GIFTS.

Anon

MY PROBLEM LIES IN RECONCILING MY GROSS HABITS WITH MY NET INCOME.

Errol Flynn

A WISE MAN SHOULD HAVE MONEY IN HIS HEAD, BUT NOT IN HIS HEART.

Jonathan Swift

IT IS BETTER TO HAVE A PERMANENT INCOME THAN TO BE FASCINATING.

Oscar Wilde

IF YOU WANT TO KNOW WHAT GOD THINKS OF MONEY, JUST LOOK AT THE PEOPLE HE GAVE IT TO.

Dorothy Parker

WHOEVER SAID MONEY CAN'T BUY HAPPINESS DIDN'T KNOW WHERE TO SHOP.

Gertrude Stein

MONEY, IF IT DOES NOT BRING YOU HAPPINESS, WILL AT LEAST HELP YOU BE MISERABLE IN COMFORT.

Helen Gurley Brown

WHERE LARGE SUMS OF MONEY ARE CONCERNED, IT IS ADVISABLE TO TRUST NOBODY.

Agatha Christie

THERE ARE PEOPLE WHO HAVE MONEY AND PEOPLE WHO ARE RICH.

Coco Chanel

WOMEN PREFER MEN WHO HAVE SOMETHING TENDER ABOUT THEM – ESPECIALLY THE LEGAL KIND.

Kay Ingram

THERE ARE PLENTY OF WAYS TO GET AHEAD. THE FIRST IS SO BASIC I'M ALMOST EMBARRASSED TO SAY IT: SPEND LESS THAN YOU EARN.

Paul Clitheroe

WE MUST BEWARE OF TRYING TO BUILD A SOCIETY IN WHICH NOBODY COUNTS FOR ANYTHING EXCEPT A POLITICIAN OR AN OFFICIAL, A SOCIETY WHERE ENTERPRISE GAINS NO REWARD AND THRIFT NO PRIVILEGES.

Winston Churchill

I BELIEVE THAT THRIFT IS ESSENTIAL TO WELL-ORDERED LIVING.

John D Rockefeller

**DON'T JUDGE EACH DAY
BY THE HARVEST YOU
REAP, BUT BY THE SEEDS
THAT YOU PLANT.**

Robert Louis Stevenson

**CANNOT PEOPLE
REALIZE HOW
LARGE AN INCOME
IS THRIFT?**

Cicero

TRAVEL

THE WORLD IS A BOOK, AND THOSE WHO DO NOT TRAVEL READ ONLY A PAGE.

St Augustine

THE WHOLE OBJECT OF TRAVEL IS NOT TO SET FOOT ON FOREIGN LAND; IT IS AT LAST TO SET FOOT ON ONE'S OWN COUNTRY AS A FOREIGN LAND.

G K Chesterton

A GOOD TRAVELLER HAS NO FIXED PLANS AND IS NOT INTENT ON ARRIVING.

Lao Tzu

WANDERING RE-ESTABLISHES THE ORIGINAL HARMONY WHICH ONCE EXISTED BETWEEN MAN AND THE UNIVERSE.

Anatole France

HOME FOR CHRISTMAS

**FOR CENTURIES
MEN HAVE KEPT AN
APPOINTMENT WITH
CHRISTMAS. CHRISTMAS
MEANS FELLOWSHIP,
FEASTING, GIVING AND
RECEIVING, A TIME OF
GOOD CHEER, HOME.**

W J Ronald Tucker

**AT CHRISTMAS, ALL
ROADS LEAD HOME.**

Marjorie Holmes

**HAPPY, HAPPY
CHRISTMAS, THAT CAN
WIN US BACK TO THE
DELUSIONS OF OUR
CHILDHOOD DAYS,
RECALL TO THE OLD MAN
THE PLEASURES OF HIS
YOUTH, AND TRANSPORT
THE TRAVELLER BACK
TO HIS OWN FIRESIDE
AND QUIET HOME!**

Charles Dickens

I'M NOT GOING TO VACUUM TILL SEARS MAKES ONE YOU CAN RIDE ON.

Roseanne Barr

DON'T COOK. DON'T CLEAN. NO MAN WILL EVER MAKE LOVE TO A WOMAN BECAUSE SHE WAXED THE LINOLEUM – 'MY GOD, THE FLOOR'S IMMACULATE. LIE DOWN, YOU HOT BITCH.'

Joan Rivers

**MY THEORY ON
HOUSEWORK IS, IF
THE ITEM DOESN'T
MULTIPLY, SMELL, CATCH
FIRE, OR BLOCK THE
REFRIGERATOR DOOR,
LET IT BE. NO ONE
ELSE CARES. WHY
SHOULD YOU?**

Erma Bombeck

**THEY'RE SURE
HOUSEWORK WON'T
KILL YOU, BUT WHY
TAKE THE RISK?**

Anon

SHOW ME A MAN WHO LIVES ALONE AND HAS A PERPETUALLY CLEAN KITCHEN, AND 8 TIMES OUT OF 9 I'LL SHOW YOU A MAN WITH DETESTABLE SPIRITUAL QUALITIES.

Charles Bukowski

ONE ONLY NEEDS TWO TOOLS IN LIFE: WD-40 TO MAKE THINGS GO, AND DUCT TAPE TO MAKE THEM STOP.

G M Weilacher

DO YOU KNOW WHAT IT MEANS TO COME HOME AT NIGHT TO A WOMAN WHO'LL GIVE YOU A LITTLE LOVE, A LITTLE AFFECTION, A LITTLE TENDERNESS? IT MEANS YOU'RE IN THE WRONG HOUSE, THAT'S WHAT IT *MEANS*.

Henry Youngman

MANY A MAN WHO
THINKS TO FOUND A
HOME DISCOVERS THAT
HE HAS MERELY OPENED
A TAVERN FOR HIS
FRIENDS.

Norman Douglas

DECK THE HALLS

NO MATTER HOW CAREFULLY YOU STORED THE LIGHTS LAST YEAR, THEY WILL BE SNARLED AGAIN THIS CHRISTMAS.

Robert Kirby

TINSEL IS REALLY SNAKES' MIRRORS.

Steven Wright

**NEVER WORRY ABOUT
THE SIZE OF YOUR
CHRISTMAS TREE. IN THE
EYES OF CHILDREN, THEY
ARE ALL 30 FEET TALL.**

Larry Wilde

**PERHAPS THE BEST
YULETIDE DECORATION
IS BEING WREATHED
IN SMILES.**

Anon

SNOW

A GREEN CHRISTMAS MAKES A FAT CHURCHYARD.

English proverb

THE AGEING PROCESS HAS YOU FIRMLY IN ITS GRASP IF YOU NEVER GET THE URGE TO THROW A SNOWBALL.

Doug Larson

**THE FIRST FALL OF
SNOW IS NOT ONLY AN
EVENT, IT IS A MAGICAL
EVENT. YOU GO TO BED
IN ONE KIND OF A
WORLD AND WAKE UP
IN ANOTHER QUITE
DIFFERENT, AND IF THIS
IS NOT ENCHANTMENT
THEN WHERE IS IT
TO BE FOUND?**

J B Priestley

THERE'S ONE GOOD THING ABOUT SNOW, IT MAKES YOUR LAWN LOOK AS NICE AS YOUR NEIGHBOUR'S.

Clyde Moore

CHRISTMAS
EVE

THERE ARE NO STRANGERS ON CHRISTMAS EVE.

George Melton (Harry Carey)
in 'Beyond Tomorow'

LET'S BE NAUGHTY AND SAVE SANTA THE TRIP.

Gary Allen

IT'S CHRISTMAS EVE. IT'S THE ONE NIGHT OF THE YEAR WHEN WE ALL ACT A LITTLE NICER, WE SMILE A LITTLE EASIER, WE CHEER A LITTLE MORE. FOR A COUPLE OF HOURS OUT OF THE WHOLE YEAR WE ARE THE PEOPLE THAT WE ALWAYS HOPED WE WOULD BE.

Frank Cross (Bill Murray) in 'Scrooged'

SANTA

THE MAIN REASON SANTA IS SO JOLLY IS BECAUSE HE KNOWS WHERE ALL THE BAD GIRLS LIVE.

George Carlin

YOU KNOW YOU'RE GETTING OLD, WHEN SANTA STARTS LOOKING YOUNGER.

Robert Paul

WHY IS CHRISTMAS JUST LIKE A DAY AT THE OFFICE? YOU DO ALL THE WORK AND THE FAT GUY WITH THE SUIT GETS ALL THE CREDIT.

Anon

THERE ARE THREE STAGES OF MAN: HE BELIEVES IN SANTA CLAUS; HE DOES NOT BELIEVE IN SANTA CLAUS; HE IS SANTA CLAUS.

Bob Phillips

WHAT DO YOU CALL PEOPLE WHO ARE AFRAID OF SANTA CLAUS? CLAUSTROPHOBIC.

Anon

THE
GIVING...

NOTHING'S AS MEAN AS GIVING A LITTLE CHILD SOMETHING USEFUL FOR CHRISTMAS.

Kin Hubbard

WE SHOULD GIVE AS WE WOULD RECEIVE, CHEERFULLY, QUICKLY, AND WITHOUT HESITATION; FOR THERE IS NO GRACE IN A BENEFIT THAT STICKS TO THE FINGERS.

Seneca

GUILT: THE GIFT THAT KEEPS ON GIVING.

Erma Bombeck

MAIL YOUR PACKAGES EARLY SO THE POST OFFICE CAN LOSE THEM IN TIME FOR CHRISTMAS.

Johnny Carson

**EVERY GIFT WHICH IS
GIVEN, EVEN THOUGH IT
BE SMALL, IS IN REALITY
GREAT, IF IT IS GIVEN
WITH AFFECTION.**

Pindar

**ANYONE WHO BELIEVES
THAT MEN ARE THE
EQUAL OF WOMEN HAS
NEVER SEEN A MAN
TRYING TO WRAP
A CHRISTMAS PRESENT.**

Anon

PRESENTS ARE THE BEST WAY TO SHOW SOMEONE HOW MUCH YOU CARE. IT IS LIKE THIS TANGIBLE THING THAT YOU CAN POINT TO AND SAY 'HEY MAN, I LOVE YOU THIS MANY DOLLARS WORTH.'

Michael Scott (Steve Carell) in 'The Office'

...AND THE
RECEIVING
OF GIFTS

THE ONE THING WOMEN DON'T WANT TO FIND IN THEIR STOCKINGS ON CHRISTMAS MORNING IS THEIR HUSBAND.

Joan Rivers

IN SUGGESTING GIFTS: MONEY IS APPROPRIATE, AND ONE SIZE FITS ALL.

William Randolph Hearst

PRESENTS, I OFTEN SAY, ENDEAR ABSENTS.

Charles Lamb

CHILDREN

THERE'S NOTHING SADDER IN THIS WORLD THAN TO AWAKE CHRISTMAS MORNING AND NOT BE A CHILD.

Erma Bombeck

CHRISTMAS TO A CHILD IS THE FIRST TERRIBLE PROOF THAT TO TRAVEL HOPEFULLY IS BETTER THAN TO ARRIVE,

Stephen Fry

NO SELF-RESPECTING MOTHER WOULD RUN OUT OF INTIMIDATIONS ON THE EVE OF A MAJOR HOLIDAY.

Erma Bombeck

THREE PHRASES THAT SUM UP CHRISTMAS ARE: PEACE ON EARTH, GOODWILL TO MEN, AND BATTERIES NOT INCLUDED.

Anon

A CHILD THAT'S BORN ON A CHRISTMAS DAY, IS FAIR AND WISE, GOOD AND GAY.

English proverb

LEARNING TO DISLIKE CHILDREN AT AN EARLY AGE SAVES A LOT OF EXPENSE AND AGGRAVATION LATER IN LIFE.

Robert Byrne

NEVER RAISE YOUR HAND TO YOUR CHILDREN; IT LEAVES YOUR MIDSECTION UNPROTECTED.

Robert Orben

TO BRING UP A CHILD IN THE WAY HE SHOULD GO, TRAVEL THAT WAY YOURSELF ONCE IN A WHILE.

Josh Billings

CHILDREN ARE
A GREAT COMFORT
IN YOUR OLD AGE
– AND THEY HELP YOU
REACH IT FASTER, TOO.

Lionel Kauffman

YOU CAN LEARN MANY
THINGS FROM CHILDREN.
HOW MUCH PATIENCE
YOU HAVE, FOR
INSTANCE.

Franklin P Jones

NEVER LEND YOUR CAR TO ANYONE TO WHOM YOU HAVE GIVEN BIRTH.

Erma Bombeck

LOVING A CHILD DOESN'T MEAN GIVING IN TO ALL HIS WHIMS; TO LOVE HIM IS TO BRING OUT THE BEST IN HIM, TO TEACH HIM TO LOVE WHAT IS DIFFICULT.

Nadia Boulanger

THERE IS ONLY ONE PRETTY CHILD IN THE WORLD, AND EVERY MOTHER HAS IT.

Chinese proverb

DO NOT, ON A RAINY DAY, ASK YOUR CHILD WHAT HE FEELS LIKE DOING, BECAUSE I ASSURE YOU THAT WHAT HE FEELS LIKE DOING, YOU WON'T FEEL LIKE WATCHING.

Fran Lebowitz

CHILDREN ARE OUR SECOND CHANCE TO HAVE A GREAT PARENT–CHILD RELATIONSHIP.

Laura Schlessinger

THE FINEST INHERITANCE YOU CAN GIVE TO A CHILD IS TO ALLOW IT TO MAKE ITS OWN WAY, COMPLETELY ON ITS OWN FEET.

Isadora Duncan

YOU SEE MUCH MORE OF YOUR CHILDREN ONCE THEY LEAVE HOME.

Lucille Ball

BOYHOOD, LIKE MEASLES, IS ONE OF THOSE COMPLAINTS WHICH A MAN SHOULD CATCH YOUNG AND HAVE DONE WITH, FOR WHEN IT COMES IN MIDDLE LIFE IT IS APT TO BE SERIOUS.

P G Wodehouse

YOUTH TROUBLES OVER ETERNITY, AGE GRASPS AT A DAY AND IS SATISFIED TO HAVE EVEN THE DAY.

Dame Mary Gilmore

YOUTH IS A DISEASE FROM WHICH WE ALL RECOVER.

Dorothy Fulheim

REMEMBER THAT AS A TEENAGER YOU ARE AT THE LAST STAGE IN YOUR LIFE WHEN YOU WILL BE HAPPY TO HEAR THAT THE PHONE IS FOR YOU.

Fran Lebowitz

KEEP TRUE TO THE DREAMS OF YOUR YOUTH.

Friedrich Schiller

TOO CHASTE A YOUTH LEADS TO A DISSOLUTE OLD AGE.

André Gide

THE
BETTER
HALF

AN OBJECT IN POSSESSION SELDOM RETAINS THE SAME CHARM THAT IT HAD IN PURSUIT.

Pliny the Younger

WHEN A MAN GIVES HIS OPINION HE'S A MAN. WHEN A WOMAN GIVES HER OPINION SHE'S A BITCH.

Bette Davis

MARRIAGE IS A GREAT INSTITUTION, BUT I'M NOT READY FOR AN INSTITUTION YET.

Mae West

A GOOD HUSBAND IS HEALTHY AND ABSENT.

Japanese proverb

I MARRIED BENEATH ME; ALL WOMEN DO.

Nancy Astor

A MAN WOULD PREFER TO COME HOME TO AN UNMADE BED AND A HAPPY WOMAN THAN TO A NEATLY MADE BED AND AN ANGRY WOMAN.

Marlene Dietrich

HAPPINESS IN MARRIAGE IS ENTIRELY A MATTER OF CHANCE.

Jane Austen

WHATEVER YOU MAY LOOK LIKE, MARRY A MAN YOUR OWN AGE – AS YOUR BEAUTY FADES, SO WILL HIS EYESIGHT.

Phyllis Diller

CAN YOU IMAGINE A WORLD WITHOUT MEN? NO CRIME AND LOTS OF HAPPY FAT WOMEN.

Nicole Hollander

THE ONLY TIME A WOMAN REALLY SUCCEEDS IN CHANGING A MAN IS WHEN HE IS A BABY.

Natalie Wood

NO ONE SHOULD HAVE TO DANCE BACKWARD ALL OF THEIR LIVES.

Jill Ruckelshaus

IN PASSING, ALSO, I WOULD LIKE TO SAY THAT THE FIRST TIME ADAM HAD A CHANCE, HE LAID THE BLAME ON A WOMAN.

Nancy Astor

WHEN A MAN STEALS YOUR WIFE, THERE IS NO BETTER REVENGE THAN TO LET HIM KEEP HER.

Sacha Guitry

GIVE UP ALL HOPE OF PEACE SO LONG AS YOUR MOTHER-IN-LAW IS ALIVE.

Juvenal

NEVER MARRY
FOR MONEY.
YE'LL BORROW
IT CHEAPER.

Scottish proverb

FRIENDS AND FAMILY

VISITS ALWAYS GIVE PLEASURE – IF NOT THE ARRIVAL, THE DEPARTURE.

Portuguese proverb

SANTA CLAUS HAS THE RIGHT IDEA – VISIT PEOPLE ONLY ONCE A YEAR.

Victor Borge

**WHEN OUR RELATIVES
ARE AT HOME, WE HAVE
TO THINK OF ALL THEIR
GOOD POINTS OR IT
WOULD BE IMPOSSIBLE
TO ENDURE THEM.**

George Bernard Shaw

**HAPPINESS IS
HAVING A LARGE,
LOVING, CARING,
CLOSE-KNIT FAMILY
IN ANOTHER CITY.**

George Burns

FISH AND VISITORS SMELL IN THREE DAYS.

Benjamin Franklin

FAMILIES ARE LIKE FUDGE – MOSTLY SWEET WITH A FEW NUTS.

Anon

IF YOU CANNOT GET RID OF THE FAMILY SKELETON, YOU MAY AS WELL MAKE IT DANCE.

George Bernard Shaw

PEOPLE REALLY ACT WEIRD AT CHRISTMAS TIME! WHAT OTHER TIME OF YEAR DO YOU SIT IN FRONT OF A DEAD TREE IN THE LIVING ROOM AND EAT NUTS AND SWEETS OUT OF YOUR SOCKS?

Anon

CALL IT A CLAN, CALL IT A NETWORK, CALL IT A TRIBE, CALL IT A FAMILY. WHATEVER YOU CALL IT, WHOEVER YOU ARE, YOU NEED ONE.

Jane Howard

IT IS A NATURAL VIRTUE INCIDENT TO OUR SEX TO BE PITIFUL OF THOSE THAT ARE AFFLICTED.

Elizabeth I

**OF ALL THE THINGS THAT
WISDOM PROVIDES TO
HELP ONE LIVE ONE'S
ENTIRE LIFE IN
HAPPINESS, THE
GREATEST BY FAR IS
THE POSSESSION OF
FRIENDSHIP. EATING OR
DRINKING WITHOUT A
FRIEND IS THE LIFE OF
A LION OR A WOLF.**

Epicurus

YOU CAN MAKE MORE FRIENDS IN TWO MONTHS BY BECOMING INTERESTED IN OTHER PEOPLE THAN YOU CAN IN TWO YEARS BY TRYING TO GET PEOPLE INTERESTED IN YOU.

Dale Carnegie

TRUE FRIENDS STAB YOU IN THE FRONT.

Oscar Wilde

YOU CAN ALWAYS TELL A REAL FRIEND: WHEN YOU'VE MADE A FOOL OF YOURSELF HE DOESN'T FEEL YOU'VE DONE A PERMANENT JOB.

Laurence J Peter

WHEN YOU CHOOSE YOUR FRIENDS, DON'T BE SHORT-CHANGED BY CHOOSING PERSONALITY OVER CHARACTER.

W Somerset Maugham

IF A MAN DOES NOT MAKE NEW ACQUAINTANCES AS HE ADVANCES THROUGH LIFE, HE WILL SOON FIND HIMSELF ALONE. A MAN SHOULD KEEP HIS FRIENDSHIPS IN CONSTANT REPAIR.

Dr Johnson

IF YOU JUDGE PEOPLE, YOU HAVE NO TIME TO LOVE THEM.

Mother Teresa

**MEN KICK FRIENDSHIP
AROUND LIKE A
FOOTBALL BUT IT
DOESN'T SEEM TO
BREAK. WOMEN TREAT
IT LIKE GLASS AND IT
GOES TO PIECES.**

Anne Morrow Lindbergh

**FRIENDSHIP IS NOT
POSSIBLE BETWEEN TWO
WOMEN, ONE OF WHOM
IS VERY WELL DRESSED.**

Laurie Colwin

IT IS THE FRIENDS YOU CAN CALL UP AT 4 A.M. THAT MATTER.

Marlene Dietrich

WHERE THERE IS GREAT LOVE THERE ARE ALWAYS MIRACLES.

Willa Cather

MORE THAN SANTA CLAUS, YOUR SISTER KNOWS WHEN YOU'VE BEEN BAD AND GOOD.

Linda Sunshine

LOOK FOR THE GOOD, NOT THE EVIL, IN THE CONDUCT OF MEMBERS OF THE FAMILY.

Proverb

**REMEMBER, BLOOD
IS NOT ONLY MUCH
THICKER THAN WATER,
IT'S MUCH MORE
DIFFICULT TO GET
OUT OF THE CARPET.**

Phyllis Diller

THE
TURKEY

A TURKEY NEVER VOTED FOR AN EARLY CHRISTMAS.

Irish proverb

MOST TURKEYS TASTE BETTER THE DAY AFTER; MY MOTHER'S TASTED BETTER THE DAY BEFORE.

Rita Rudner

FOOD

**CHRISTMAS ITSELF
MAY BE CALLED
INTO QUESTION, IF
CARRIED SO FAR
IT CREATES
INDIGESTION.**

Ralph Bergengren

**THE WORST GIFT IS A
FRUITCAKE. THERE IS
ONLY ONE FRUITCAKE
IN THE ENTIRE WORLD,
AND PEOPLE KEEP
SENDING IT TO
EACH OTHER.**

Johnny Carson

I TRUST CHRISTMAS BRINGS TO YOU ITS TRADITIONAL MIX OF GOOD FOOD AND VIOLENT STOMACH CRAMPS.

Ebenezer Blackadder (Rowan Atkinson)
in 'Blackadder's Christmas Carol'

EAT AND DRINK ON CHRISTMAS – FOR EASTER, NEW CLOTHING.

Irish proverb

DRINK

THE PROPER BEHAVIOUR ALL THROUGH THE HOLIDAY SEASON IS TO BE DRUNK. THIS DRUNKENNESS CULMINATES ON NEW YEAR'S EVE, WHEN YOU GET SO DRUNK YOU KISS THE PERSON YOU'RE MARRIED TO.

P J O'Rourke

SOMETIMES TOO MUCH TO DRINK IS BARELY ENOUGH.

Mark Twain

DO NOT ALLOW CHILDREN TO MIX DRINKS. IT IS UNSEEMLY AND THEY USE TOO MUCH VERMOUTH.

Steve Allen

THERE'S NOTHING LIKE A COLD BEER ON A HOT CHRISTMAS MORNING.

Homer Simpson

OVER-
INDULGENCE

PEOPLE ARE SO WORRIED ABOUT WHAT THEY EAT BETWEEN CHRISTMAS AND THE NEW YEAR, BUT THEY REALLY SHOULD BE WORRIED ABOUT WHAT THEY EAT BETWEEN THE NEW YEAR AND CHRISTMAS.

Anon

DYSPEPSIA IS THE REMORSE OF A GUILTY STOMACH.

A Kerr

IF YOUR STOMACH DISPUTES YOU, LIE DOWN AND PACIFY IT WITH COOL THOUGHTS.

Satchel Paige

EAT, DRINK, AND BE MERRY, FOR TOMORROW YE DIET.

William Gilmore Beymer

IT IS EXERCISE ALONE THAT SUPPORTS THE SPIRITS, AND KEEPS THE MIND IN VIGOUR.

Cicero

EXERCISE IS A DIRTY WORD. EVERY TIME I HEAR IT, I WASH MY MOUTH OUT WITH CHOCOLATE.

Anon

IF GOD HAD WANTED US TO BEND OVER, HE WOULD HAVE PUT DIAMONDS ON THE FLOOR.

Joan Rivers

MY IDEA OF EXERCISE IS A GOOD BRISK SIT.

Phyllis Diller

IF YOU HAVE FORMED THE HABIT OF CHECKING ON EVERY NEW DIET THAT COMES ALONG, YOU WILL FIND THAT, MERCIFULLY, THEY ALL BLUR TOGETHER, LEAVING YOU WITH ONLY ONE DEFINITE PIECE OF INFORMATION: FRENCH-FRIED POTATOES ARE OUT.

Jean Kerr

**THE CHIEF EXCITEMENT
IN A WOMAN'S LIFE IS
SPOTTING WOMEN WHO
ARE FATTER THAN SHE IS.**

Helen Rowland

**RICH, FATTY FOODS ARE
LIKE DESTINY: THEY TOO,
SHAPE OUR ENDS.**

Anon

NEVER EAT MORE THAN YOU CAN LIFT.

Miss Piggy

FIVE DAYS SHALT THOU LABOUR, AS THE BIBLE SAYS. THE SEVENTH DAY IS THE LORD THY GOD'S. THE SIXTH DAY IS FOR FOOTBALL.

Anthony Burgess

I BELIEVE THAT THE GOOD LORD GAVE US A FINITE NUMBER OF HEARTBEATS AND I'M DAMNED IF I'M GOING TO USE UP MINE RUNNING UP AND DOWN A STREET.

Neil Armstrong

LIFE IS UNCERTAIN. EAT DESSERT FIRST.

Ernestine Ulmer

CHRISTMAS
TV

OH LOOK, YET ANOTHER
CHRISTMAS TV SPECIAL!
HOW TOUCHING TO HAVE
THE MEANING OF
CHRISTMAS BROUGHT
TO US BY COLA, FAST
FOOD, AND BEER...
WHO'D HAVE EVER
GUESSED THAT PRODUCT
CONSUMPTION, POPULAR
ENTERTAINMENT, AND
SPIRITUALITY WOULD
MIX SO HARMONIOUSLY?

Calvin and Hobbes

IF GOD HAD MEANT CHRISTMAS TO BE A FAMILY OCCASION HE WOULDN'T HAVE INVENTED TV, WOULD HE?

Rory McGrath

GOODWILL
TO ALL
MEN

CHRISTMAS IS THE SEASON FOR KINDLING THE FIRE OF HOSPITALITY IN THE HALL, THE GENIAL FLAME OF CHARITY IN THE HEART.

Washington Irving

IF YOU HAVEN'T GOT ANY CHARITY IN YOUR HEART, YOU HAVE THE WORST KIND OF HEART TROUBLE.

Bob Hope

**REMEMBER, IF
CHRISTMAS ISN'T
FOUND IN YOUR HEART,
YOU WON'T FIND IT
UNDER A TREE.**

Charlotte Carpenter

**I WISH WE COULD
PUT UP SOME OF THE
CHRISTMAS SPIRIT IN
JARS AND OPEN A JAR
OF IT EVERY MONTH.**

Harlan Miller

ONE OF THE NICE THINGS ABOUT CHRISTMAS IS THAT YOU CAN MAKE PEOPLE FORGET THE PAST WITH A PRESENT.

Anon

UNLESS WE MAKE CHRISTMAS AN OCCASION TO SHARE OUR BLESSINGS, ALL THE SNOW IN ALASKA WON'T MAKE IT 'WHITE'.

Bing Crosby

**CHRISTMAS GIFT
SUGGESTIONS: TO YOUR
ENEMY, FORGIVENESS.
TO AN OPPONENT,
TOLERANCE. TO A
FRIEND, YOUR HEART. TO
A CUSTOMER, SERVICE.
TO ALL, CHARITY.
TO EVERY CHILD,
A GOOD EXAMPLE.
TO YOURSELF, RESPECT.**

Oren Arnold

MANNERS MAKETH MAN.

William of Wykeham

CHRISTMAS IS NOT A TIME NOR A SEASON, BUT A STATE OF MIND. TO CHERISH PEACE AND GOODWILL, TO BE PLENTEOUS IN MERCY, IS TO HAVE THE REAL SPIRIT OF CHRISTMAS.

Calvin Coolidge

A GENTLEMAN IS ANY MAN WHO WOULDN'T HIT A WOMAN WITH HIS HAT ON.

Fred Allen

**IT IS NOT EASY TO
FIND HAPPINESS IN
OURSELVES, AND IT IS
NOT POSSIBLE TO FIND
IT ELSEWHERE.**

Agnes Repplier

**TO BE KIND TO ALL, TO
LIKE MANY AND LOVE A
FEW, TO BE NEEDED AND
WANTED BY THOSE WE
LOVE, IS CERTAINLY THE
NEAREST WE CAN COME
TO HAPPINESS.**

Mary, Queen of Scots

HAPPINESS IS NOT A GOAL; IT IS A BY-PRODUCT.

Eleanor Roosevelt

WHY NOT SEIZE THE PLEASURE AT ONCE, HOW OFTEN IS HAPPINESS DESTROYED BY PREPARATION, FOOLISH PREPARATIONS.

Jane Austen

IT IS ONLY POSSIBLE TO LIVE HAPPILY EVER AFTER ON A DAY-TO-DAY BASIS.

Margaret Bonnano

HAPPINESS MUST BE CULTIVATED. IT IS LIKE CHARACTER. IT IS NOT A THING TO BE SAFELY LET ALONE FOR A MOMENT, OR IT WILL RUN TO WEEDS.

Elizabeth Stuart Phelps

A GENTLEMAN CAN LIVE THROUGH ANYTHING.

William Faulkner

THE ONLY INFALLIBLE RULE WE KNOW IS, THAT THE MAN WHO IS ALWAYS TALKING ABOUT BEING A GENTLEMAN NEVER IS ONE.

Robert Smith Surtees

BAH
HUMBUG

CHRISTMAS IS A TIME WHEN YOU GET HOMESICK – EVEN WHEN YOU'RE HOME.

Carol Nelson

'A MERRY CHRISTMAS, UNCLE! GOD SAVE YOU!' CRIED A CHEERFUL VOICE. 'BAH' SAID SCROOGE. 'HUMBUG!'

Charles Dickens

A SEVERED FOOT IS THE PERFECT STOCKING STUFFER.

Mitch Hedberg

BAH! HOW HOLLOW IT ALL IS! ALWAYS ON CHRISTMAS, THOUGH, I FEEL MY OWN HEART SOFTEN – TOWARD THE LATE JUDAS ISCARIOT.

Ambrose Bierce

BLAST THIS CHRISTMAS MUSIC. IT'S JOYFUL AND TRIUMPHANT.

Grinch (Jim Carrey) in
'How the Grinch Stole Christmas'

MERRY CHRISTMAS, NEARLY EVERYBODY!

Ogden Nash

MEN WHO ARE UNHAPPY, LIKE MEN WHO SLEEP BADLY, ARE ALWAYS PROUD OF THE FACT.

Bertrand Russell

START OFF EVERY DAY WITH A SMILE AND GET IT OVER WITH.

W C Fields

YOU NEVER REALLY KNOW YOUR FRIENDS FROM YOUR ENEMIES UNTIL THE ICE BREAKS.

Eskimo proverb

NEVER INTERRUPT YOUR ENEMY WHEN HE IS MAKING A MISTAKE.

Napoleon Bonaparte

FORGIVE YOUR ENEMIES, BUT NEVER FORGET THEIR NAMES.

John F Kennedy

EVERYONE NEEDS A WARM PERSONAL ENEMY OR TWO TO KEEP HIM FREE FROM RUST IN THE MOVABLE PARTS OF HIS MIND.

Gene Fowler

THE FIRST HALF OF OUR LIVES IS RUINED BY OUR PARENTS, AND THE SECOND HALF BY OUR CHILDREN.

Clarence Darrow

I HAVE ALWAYS DISLIKED MYSELF AT ANY GIVEN MOMENT; THE TOTAL OF SUCH MOMENTS IS MY LIFE.

Cyril Connolly

PATIENCE, N.
A MINOR FORM OF
DESPAIR, DISGUISED
AS A VIRTUE.

Ambrose Bierce

A CYNIC IS A MAN WHO,
WHEN HE SMELLS
FLOWERS, LOOKS
AROUND FOR
A COFFIN.

H L Mencken

ASK YOURSELF WHETHER YOU ARE HAPPY, AND YOU CEASE TO BE SO.

John Stuart Mill

NOBODY REALLY CARES IF YOU'RE MISERABLE, SO YOU MIGHT AS WELL BE HAPPY.

Cynthia Nelms

AND YET TO EVERY BAD THERE IS A WORSE.

Thomas Hardy

LUXURY: THE LUST FOR COMFORT, THAT STEALTHY THING THAT ENTERS THE HOUSE AS A GUEST, AND THEN BECOMES A HOST, AND THEN A MASTER.

Kahlil Gibran

THE DARKEST HOUR IN ANY MAN'S LIFE IS WHEN HE SITS DOWN TO PLAN HOW TO GET MONEY WITHOUT EARNING IT.

Horace Greeley

HAPPINESS, N. AN AGREEABLE SENSATION ARISING FROM CONTEMPLATING THE MISERY OF ANOTHER.

Ambrose Bierce

HAPPINESS IS A PERPETUAL POSSESSION OF BEING WELL DECEIVED.

Jonathan Swift

WE ARE MORE INTERESTED IN MAKING OTHERS BELIEVE WE ARE HAPPY THAN IN TRYING TO BE HAPPY OURSELVES.

François de La Rochefoucauld

**WE WISH TO BE HAPPIER
THAN OTHER PEOPLE;
AND THIS IS ALWAYS
DIFFICULT, FOR WE
BELIEVE OTHERS TO
BE HAPPIER THAN
THEY ARE.**

Charles-Louis de Secondat baron de Montesquieu

**POINT ME OUT THE
HAPPY MAN AND I WILL
POINT YOU OUT EITHER
EGOTISM, SELFISHNESS,
EVIL – OR ELSE AN
ABSOLUTE IGNORANCE.**

Graham Greene

WHAT A WONDERFUL LIFE I'VE HAD! I ONLY WISH I'D REALISED IT SOONER.

Colette

I'M AN OPTIMIST, BUT I'M AN OPTIMIST WHO CARRIES A RAINCOAT.

Harold Wilson

CALL NO MAN HAPPY TILL HE IS DEAD.

Aeschylus

FOR A GREEDY MAN EVEN HIS TOMB IS TOO SMALL.

Tajikistani proverb

COMFORT
AND JOY

A LOVELY THING ABOUT CHRISTMAS IS THAT IT'S COMPULSORY, LIKE A THUNDERSTORM, AND WE ALL GO THROUGH IT TOGETHER.

Garrison Keillor

AT CHRISTMAS PLAY AND MAKE GOOD CHEER, FOR CHRISTMAS COMES BUT ONCE A YEAR.

Thomas Tusser

GIFTS OF TIME AND LOVE ARE SURELY THE BASIC INGREDIENTS OF A TRULY MERRY CHRISTMAS.

Peg Bracken

CHRISTMAS IS A BRIDGE. WE NEED BRIDGES AS THE RIVER OF TIME FLOWS PAST. TODAY'S CHRISTMAS SHOULD MEAN CREATING HAPPY HOURS FOR TOMORROW AND RELIVING THOSE OF YESTERDAY.

Gladys Taber

THERE IS MORE
TO LIFE THAN
INCREASING
ITS SPEED.

Mahatma Gandhi

HAPPINESS DEPENDS
UPON OURSELVES.

Aristotle

TO BE WITHOUT SOME OF THE THINGS YOU WANT IS AN INDISPENSABLE PART OF HAPPINESS.

Bertrand Russell

THE FOOLISH MAN SEEKS HAPPINESS IN THE DISTANCE, THE WISE GROWS IT UNDER HIS FEET.

James Oppenheim

**HAPPINESS IS NOTHING
MORE THAN GOOD
HEALTH AND A
BAD MEMORY.**

Albert Schweitzer

**NOW AND THEN IT'S
GOOD TO PAUSE IN OUR
PURSUIT OF HAPPINESS
AND JUST BE HAPPY.**

Guillaume Apollinaire

WE DEEM THOSE HAPPY WHO FROM THE EXPERIENCE OF LIFE HAVE LEARNED TO BEAR ITS ILLS, WITHOUT BEING OVERCOME BY THEM.

Juvenal

TO BE HAPPY FOR AN HOUR, GET DRUNK; TO BE HAPPY FOR A YEAR, FALL IN LOVE; TO BE HAPPY FOR LIFE, TAKE UP GARDENING.

Chinese proverb

A LIFETIME OF HAPPINESS! NO MAN ALIVE COULD BEAR IT: IT WOULD BE HELL ON EARTH.

George Bernard Shaw

OUR LIFE IS FRITTERED AWAY BY DETAIL. SIMPLIFY, SIMPLIFY.

Henry David Thoreau

IF YOU CAN SPEND A PERFECTLY USELESS AFTERNOON IN A PERFECTLY USELESS MANNER, YOU HAVE LEARNED HOW TO LIVE.

Lin Yutang

USE YOUR HEALTH, EVEN TO THE POINT OF WEARING IT OUT. THAT IS WHAT IT IS FOR. SPEND ALL YOU HAVE BEFORE YOU DIE; DO NOT OUTLIVE YOURSELF.

George Bernard Shaw

THE BEST PORTION OF A GOOD MAN'S LIFE – HIS LITTLE, NAMELESS, UNREMEMBERED ACTS OF KINDNESS.

William Wordsworth

ALWAYS BE KIND, FOR EVERYONE IS FIGHTING A HARD BATTLE.

Plato

RELIGION

HOW MANY OBSERVE CHRIST'S BIRTHDAY! HOW FEW, HIS PRECEPTS! O! 'TIS EASIER TO KEEP HOLIDAYS THAN COMMANDMENTS.

Benjamin Franklin

THIS IS THE MESSAGE OF CHRISTMAS: WE ARE NEVER ALONE.

Taylor Caldwell

WHEN WE WERE CHILDREN WE WERE GRATEFUL TO THOSE WHO FILLED OUR STOCKINGS AT CHRISTMAS TIME. WHY ARE WE NOT GRATEFUL TO GOD FOR FILLING OUR STOCKINGS WITH LEGS?

G K Chesterton

THE CHRISTMAS TREE HAS TAKEN THE PLACE OF THE ALTAR IN TOO MUCH OF OUR MODERN CHRISTMAS OBSERVANCE.

Anon

CHRISTMAS WAVES A MAGIC WAND OVER THIS WORLD, AND BEHOLD, EVERYTHING IS SOFTER AND MORE BEAUTIFUL.

Norman Vincent Peale

ROSES ARE REDDISH
VIOLETS ARE BLUISH
IF IT WEREN'T FOR
CHRISTMAS WE'D
ALL BE JEWISH.

Benny Hill

SPIRIT OF CHRISTMAS

NEXT TO A CIRCUS THERE AIN'T NOTHING THAT PACKS UP AND TEARS OUT FASTER THAN THE CHRISTMAS SPIRIT.

Kin Hubbard

AT CHRISTMAS I NO MORE DESIRE A ROSE, THAN WISH A SNOW IN MAY'S NEW-FANGLED SHOWS; BUT LIKE OF EACH THING THAT IN SEASON GROWS.

William Shakespeare

**CHRISTMAS IS
NOT AS MUCH
ABOUT OPENING
OUR PRESENTS AS
OPENING OUR HEARTS.**

Janice Maeditere

**MAY WE NOT 'SPEND'
CHRISTMAS OR
'OBSERVE' CHRISTMAS,
BUT RATHER 'KEEP' IT.**

Peter Marshall

THERE IS NO IDEAL CHRISTMAS; ONLY THE ONE CHRISTMAS YOU DECIDE TO MAKE AS A REFLECTION OF YOUR VALUES, DESIRES, AFFECTIONS, TRADITIONS.

Bill McKibben

THERE MUST BE SOMETHING GHOSTLY IN THE AIR OF CHRISTMAS – SOMETHING ABOUT THE CLOSE, MUGGY ATMOSPHERE THAT DRAWS UP THE GHOSTS, LIKE THE DAMPNESS OF THE SUMMER RAINS BRINGS OUT THE FROGS AND SNAILS.

Jerome K Jerome

NEW YEAR

NEW YEAR'S IS A HARMLESS ANNUAL INSTITUTION, OF NO PARTICULAR USE TO ANYBODY SAVE AS A SCAPEGOAT FOR PROMISCUOUS DRUNKS, AND FRIENDLY CALLS AND HUMBUG RESOLUTIONS.

Mark Twain

MAY ALL YOUR TROUBLES LAST AS LONG AS YOUR NEW YEAR'S RESOLUTIONS.

Joey Adams

GOOD RESOLUTIONS ARE SIMPLY CHECKS THAT MEN DRAW ON A BANK WHERE THEY HAVE NO ACCOUNT.

Oscar Wilde

NEW YEAR'S EVE, WHERE AULD ACQUAINTANCE BE FORGOT. UNLESS, OF COURSE, THOSE TESTS COME BACK POSITIVE.

Jay Leno

NEW YEAR'S DAY... NOW IS THE ACCEPTED TIME TO MAKE YOUR REGULAR ANNUAL GOOD RESOLUTIONS. NEXT WEEK YOU CAN BEGIN PAVING HELL WITH THEM AS USUAL.

Mark Twain

YOUTH IS WHEN YOU'RE ALLOWED TO STAY UP LATE ON NEW YEAR'S EVE. MIDDLE AGE IS WHEN YOU'RE FORCED TO.

Bill Vaughan

RING OUT THE OLD, RING IN THE NEW, RING, HAPPY BELLS, ACROSS THE SNOW: THE YEAR IS GOING, LET HIM GO; RING OUT THE FALSE, RING IN THE TRUE.

Alfred Lord Tennyson

I AM AN OPTIMIST. IT DOESN'T SEEM TOO MUCH USE BEING ANYTHING ELSE.

Winston Churchill

AN OPTIMIST WILL TELL YOU THE GLASS IS HALF-FULL; THE PESSIMIST, HALF-EMPTY; AND THE ENGINEER WILL TELL YOU THE GLASS IS TWICE THE SIZE IT NEEDS TO BE.

Anon

THE FUTURE, ACCORDING TO SOME SCIENTISTS, WILL BE EXACTLY LIKE THE PAST, ONLY FAR MORE EXPENSIVE.

John Sladek

CHANGE IS INEVITABLE – EXCEPT FROM A VENDING MACHINE.

Robert Gallagher

IT IS A BAD PLAN THAT ADMITS OF NO MODIFICATION.

Syrus

STICK WITH THE OPTIMISTS. IT'S GOING TO BE TOUGH ENOUGH EVEN IF THEY'RE RIGHT.

James Reston

WHEN YOU'RE FINISHED CHANGING, YOU'RE FINISHED.

Benjamin Franklin

WHEN ONE DOOR CLOSES, ANOTHER OPENS; BUT WE OFTEN LOOK SO LONG AND SO REGRETFULLY UPON THE CLOSED DOOR THAT WE DO NOT SEE THE ONE WHICH HAS OPENED FOR US.

Alexander Graham Bell

THERE IS NO SECURITY ON THIS EARTH; THERE IS ONLY OPPORTUNITY.

General Douglas MacArthur

GATHER YE ROSEBUDS WHILE YE MAY, OLD TIME IS STILL A-FLYING. AND THIS SAME FLOWER THAT SMILES TODAY, TOMORROW WILL BE DYING.

Robert Herrick

NOTHING IS PERMANENT IN THIS WICKED WORLD – NOT EVEN OUR TROUBLES.

Charlie Chaplin

IT IS CURIOUS THAT PHYSICAL COURAGE SHOULD BE SO COMMON IN THE WORLD AND MORAL COURAGE SO RARE.

Mark Twain

IF YOU CAN FIND A PATH WITH NO OBSTACLES, IT PROBABLY DOESN'T LEAD ANYWHERE.

Frank A Clark

LUCK IS WHAT YOU HAVE LEFT OVER AFTER YOU GIVE 100 PERCENT.

Langston Coleman

SHALLOW MEN BELIEVE IN LUCK. STRONG MEN BELIEVE IN CAUSE AND EFFECT.

Ralph Waldo Emerson

I BELIEVE IN LUCK: HOW ELSE CAN YOU EXPLAIN THE SUCCESS OF THOSE YOU DISLIKE?

Jean Cocteau

DEPEND ON THE RABBIT'S FOOT IF YOU WILL, BUT REMEMBER IT DIDN'T WORK FOR THE RABBIT.

R E Shay

A GEM CANNOT BE POLISHED WITHOUT FRICTION, NOR A MAN PERFECTED WITHOUT TRIALS.

Seneca the Younger

**LET US BE OF GOOD
CHEER, REMEMBERING
THAT THE MISFORTUNES
HARDEST TO BEAR ARE
THOSE WHICH WILL
NEVER HAPPEN.**

James Russell Lowell

**IF YOU AREN'T IN OVER
YOUR HEAD, HOW DO
YOU KNOW HOW
TALL YOU ARE?**

T S Eliot

**EVEN IF YOU FALL
ON YOUR FACE, YOU'RE
STILL MOVING FORWARD.**

Robert Gallagher

**I'VE DEVELOPED A
NEW PHILOSOPHY ...
I ONLY DREAD ONE
DAY AT A TIME.**

Charlie Brown

ALWAYS BEAR IN MIND THAT YOUR OWN RESOLUTION TO SUCCEED IS MORE IMPORTANT THAN ANY ONE THING.

Abraham Lincoln

TRY NOT TO BECOME A MAN OF SUCCESS BUT RATHER TO BECOME A MAN OF VALUE.

Albert Einstein

I CAN'T GIVE YOU A SURE-FIRE FORMULA FOR SUCCESS, BUT I CAN GIVE YOU A FORMULA FOR FAILURE: TRY TO PLEASE EVERYBODY ALL THE TIME.

Herbert Bayard Swope

THE SECRET OF SUCCESS IS SINCERITY. ONCE YOU CAN FAKE THAT YOU'VE GOT IT MADE.

Jean Giraudoux

IF YOU THINK YOU CAN WIN, YOU CAN WIN. FAITH IS NECESSARY TO VICTORY.

William Hazlitt

IT IS EASY TO BE BRAVE FROM A SAFE DISTANCE.

Aesop

LET BRAVERY BE THY CHOICE, BUT NOT BRAVADO.

Menander

THE ONLY DIFFERENCE BETWEEN A RUT AND A GRAVE IS THEIR DIMENSIONS.

Ellen Glasgow

TWENTY YEARS FROM NOW YOU WILL BE MORE DISAPPOINTED BY THE THINGS THAT YOU DIDN'T DO THAN BY THE ONES YOU DID DO. SO THROW OFF THE BOWLINES. SAIL AWAY FROM SAFE HARBOR. CATCH THE TRADE WINDS IN YOUR SAILS. EXPLORE. DREAM. DISCOVER.

Mark Twain

**IT IS BETTER TO
DIE ON YOUR FEET
THAN TO LIVE ON
YOUR KNEES.**

Dolores Ibárruri

**AVOIDING DANGER
IS NO SAFER IN THE
LONG RUN THAN
OUTRIGHT EXPOSURE.
THE FEARFUL ARE
CAUGHT AS OFTEN
AS THE BOLD.**

Helen Keller

BE BOLD. IF YOU'RE GOING TO MAKE AN ERROR, MAKE A DOOZEY, AND DON'T BE AFRAID TO HIT THE BALL.

Billie Jean King

EVEN COWARDS CAN ENDURE HARDSHIP; ONLY THE BRAVE CAN ENDURE SUSPENSE.

Mignon McLaughlin

YOU CAN'T BE BRAVE IF YOU'VE ONLY HAD WONDERFUL THINGS HAPPEN TO YOU.

Mary Tyler Moore

IF YOU'RE IN A BAD SITUATION, DON'T WORRY IT'LL CHANGE. IF YOU'RE IN A GOOD SITUATION, DON'T WORRY IT'LL CHANGE.

John A Simone Sr

**IF AT FIRST YOU DON'T
SUCCEED, TRY, TRY
AGAIN. THEN QUIT.
THERE'S NO POINT IN
BEING A DAMN FOOL
ABOUT IT.**

W C Fields

**WORRY OFTEN
GIVES A SMALL THING
A BIG SHADOW.**

Swedish proverb

IF YOU CAN'T SLEEP, THEN GET UP AND DO SOMETHING INSTEAD OF LYING THERE AND WORRYING. IT'S THE WORRY THAT GETS YOU, NOT THE LOSS OF SLEEP.

Dale Carnegie

A WORRIED MAN COULD BORROW A LOT OF TROUBLE WITH PRACTICALLY NO COLLATERAL.

Helen Nielsen

DON'T WORRY ABOUT THE WORLD COMING TO AN END TODAY. IT'S ALREADY TOMORROW IN AUSTRALIA.

Charles M Schulz

HURRYING AND WORRYING ARE NOT THE SAME AS STRENGTH.

Nigerian proverb

IT AIN'T NO USE PUTTING UP YOUR UMBRELLA TILL IT RAINS.

Alice Caldwell Rice

MORE HELP
IS AT HAND...